EXPERIMENT WITH
MEASUREMENTS

DEEPANWITA CHATTOPADHYAY

Contents

1. Counting and Measuring — 3
2. Units and Standards of Measurement — 5
3. Length and Distance — 13
4. Mass and Weight — 24
5. Measuring Time — 29
6. Temperature — 33
7. Electrical Measurements — 37
   Index — 40

RISING SUN
an imprint of
New Dawn Press

NEW DAWN PRESS GROUP
New Dawn Press, Inc., 244 South Randall Rd # 90, Elgin, IL 60123
e-mail: sales@newdawnpress.com

New Dawn Press, 2 Tintern Close, Slough, Berkshire, SL1-2TB, UK
e-mail: ndpuk@newdawnpress.com
       sterlingdis@yahoo.co.uk

New Dawn Press (An Imprint of Sterling Publishers (P) Ltd.)
A-59, Okhla Industrial Area, Phase-II, New Delhi-110020
e-mail: sterlingpublishers@touchtelindia.net
       ghai@nde.vsnl.net.in

© 2005, New Dawn Press

All rights are reserved. No part of this publication may be reproduced, stored in a retrieval system or transmitted, in any form or by any means, mechanical, photocopying, recording or otherwise, without prior written permission of the publisher.

Printed at Sai Early Learners Pvt. Ltd., New Delhi-110020.

Counting and Measuring

We live in a world of numbers. Your house has a number, your telephone has a number, you have a roll number in school, your bank account has a number, pages have numbers, food items have numbers (price and weight) — practically everything you see around you is designated by a number.

Numbering is done for keeping count. Counting answers the question 'How many?'

How good are you at counting?

A box contains nails and screws. How will you tell how many nails and screws are there in the box?

You would probably separate the nails from the screws and then count them, wouldn't you? I can teach you a better way to count. All you need is a pen and paper.

1. Make two columns on the paper.
2. Start fishing out the nails and screws one by one. Each time you take out a nail put a stroke in the left column and a stroke in the right column for every screw. This stroke is called a tally mark in the opposite direction, slashing the first four.
3. Continue this till the box is empty. Then all you have to do is count the strokes in each column to know the number of nails and screws. For example, according to the diagram there are:
   $4 \times 5 + 3 =$ nails and
   $3 \times 5 = 15$ screws

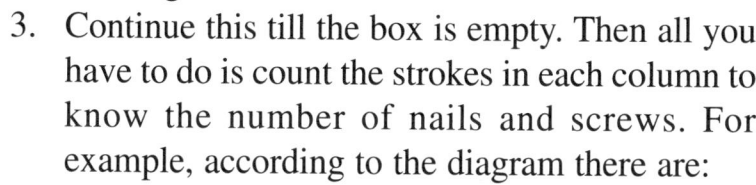

Now, if I ask you whether the box contains more nails or screws, you will compare the number of nails and screws, in this case 23 and 15, and say that there are more nails. Comparison needs a sense of sequence or order.

A comparison can be qualitative or quantitative. When we want to make quantitative comparisons, we make measurements. We measure in order to ascertain the extent or quantity of a thing by comparing it with an object of known size.

Measuring plays a very important role in our daily lives. It helps us describe things specifically. The development of science and technology depends on accurate measurements. As a student of science you should be adept at measuring. Everything from size, time, heat, sound to colour can be measured.

Measure yourself
Try and describe yourself in terms of a set of numbers. Have you mentioned the following?
- age
- height
- weight
- waist
- shoulder
- chest

Think it over
Why do you write 'metres' after height or 'kg' after weight? Can you specify weight as 32 metres? Why or why not?

Units and Standards of Measurement

When you measured your height and weight earlier, you actually compared your own height and weight with a *standard length*, called the *metre(m),* and a *standard weight,* called the *kilogram (kg).* That is, if you weighed, say, 32 kgs, it means that your weight is 32 *times* the weight of a standard kilogram.

This reference standard of measurement for a quantity is called a *unit* of that quantity. You must be familiar with the units – metres, kilograms and seconds, for length, weight and time respectively.

Does it not seem that there should be as many units as there are measurable quantities? Let us check whether it is really so, with a few examples.

Measure the area of a rectangle
1. Draw a rectangle on a piece of paper. The area of the rectangle is the space enclosed by the four lines.
2. Just as you need a *unit length* (say metre) to measure any length which is a multiple of the unit, here also you need a unit square (say 1cm x 1cm = 1cm^2) to measure the area of your rectangle.

Find out how many such *unit squares* fit your rectangle. Don't worry if there are any fractions of squares. Just add them up. The result will give you the area of the rectangle.

3. Check your result with the following formula:
   Area of a rectangle = Length x Breadth
   How well do the results match?
4. What is the unit of area? Can you derive the unit of area from the unit of length?

Unit of speed
To find out the unit of speed

You will need:
- a measuring tape
- a piece of chalk
- a stopwatch
- a friend

1. Mark out a straight track of 50 metres.
2. Ask your friend to keep time as you run the distance.
3. Now, speed is defined as the distance covered by a body in unit time.
   So, if in 6 seconds you covered 50 metres,
   in 1 second (unit time), you will cover 50/6 metres = 8.33 metres.
   Therefore your speed is 8.33 metres per second (written as m/s).

This means, like the unit of area, the unit of speed, too, can be written in terms of two known units, namely, metres and seconds.

Match the units
1. Volume   a. cm/sec^2
2. Density   b. cm^3
3. Acceleration   c. kg m/sec^2 (Newton)
4. Force   d. Nm/sec (Watt)
5. Power   e. g/cm^3

Note that all these units can be derived from the units of mass, length and time.

[**Ans:** 1-b, 2-e, 3-a, 4-c, 5-d.]

Do you know your body temperature?

You will need:
- a clinical thermometer

1. Note the markings on the body of the thermometer tube. The dark thread-like thing extending from the bulb is mercury. It expands when heated and moves along the scale. If your body is hotter than the surrounding air, the mercury in the thermometer will expand when in touch with your body. Where is the mercury level now?
2. Shake the thermometer so that the mercury level is below 96^0.
3. Wash it, and put it in your mouth.
4. Take it out after a minute and read the mercury level. The reading will correspond to your body temperature. (Our normal body temperature is $98.4^0 F$.)
5. What is the unit of temperature you read just now?

Note that unlike area and speed, temperature cannot be measured in terms of length, mass or time. Temperature has a different unit. We generally measure temperature in either degree Centigrade (^0C) or degree Fahrenheit (^0F). Scientists use Kelvin (^0K) as the temperature scale.

Did you know?
The body temperature of cold-blooded hibernators such as frogs and toads rises and falls with the temperature of the environment. When cold weather lowers their body temperature, the animals go into hibernation. They are aroused from hibernation when the environment warms up enough to heat their bodies.

Frog

Did you know?

In this way if you measured all the physical quantities in this world, you will come up with a list of the minimum convenient number of units needed for measurement.

Scientists have found that this number is seven. These are the units of length, mass, time, electric current, temperature, intensity of light and amount of substance. These units are called *basic units*.

The units of all other physical quantities, like volume, speed, force, voltage, heat, etc, can be drived from these seven basic units. That is why these units are called *derived units*.

Is it true that people all over the world use a single unit for a given thing? You can check this.

Look at your ruler

1. Note the graduations on the two edges of your ruler. Are they the same? Why not?
   The one with closer markings is called the centimetre or the metre scale (100 cms =1 metre).
   The other is called the inch or the foot scale (12 inches = 1 foot).
   This means, for measuring length, your ruler offers a choice of two units, namely 'metre' and 'foot'.
2. How many feet is a metre?
3. In the same way, take a look at a thermometer. You will find the readings given in units of centigrade as well as units of Fahrenheit.

Centimetres   Inches

Remember

'Centimetre' and 'metre' are not two different types of units. A centimetre is a division of the same unit, 'metre'. Similarly, an 'inch' is a division of the same unit, 'foot'. In scientific terminology we use the term 'mass' instead of 'weight'.

The history of the choice of units

In ancient times, the Egyptians used the distance from a *person's* elbow to the tip of the middle finger as the unit of length. This was called the *cubit*. But the cubit varied from person to person! So a 'royal cubit' was established as a standard.

The Romans adopted a different cubit, dividing it into 2 feet and each foot into 12 *unciae* (inches.) For long distances they used *millipassus,* or, one thousand paces. The mile, which is slightly longer, is based on it.

The Romans used *libra* (pound) as the standard unit of weight. That is why the pound is abbreviated as 'lb', even today.

While units for length and weight had to be established, time has natural keepers, like the sun and the moon, that fix the durations of the year and the day. Nearly 5,000 years ago, Babylonian astronomers divided the day into 24 equal hours. Each hour in turn was divided into 60 equal minutes, and each minute into 60 seconds.

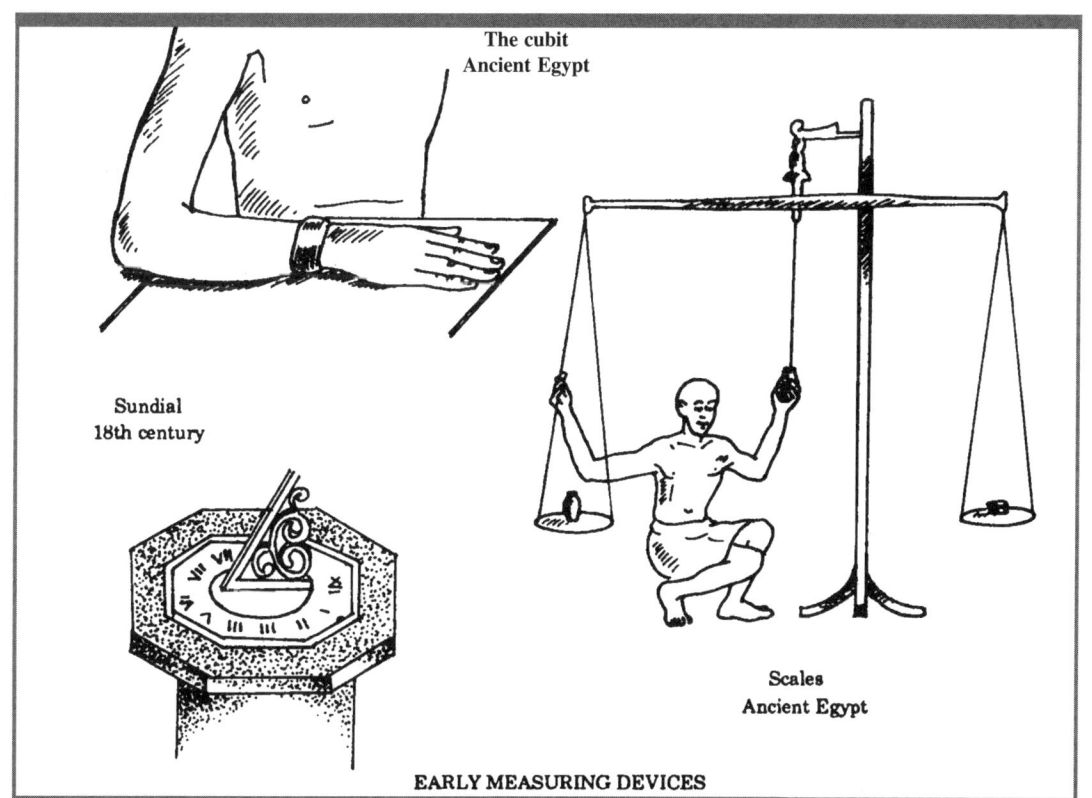

EARLY MEASURING DEVICES

The present standards

In the 1790s, a commission of French scientists developed the *metric system*. It was based on a length unit called the *metre* which is one ten-millionth of the distance between the poles and the equator, measured along the meridian through Dunkirk in France. Larger and smaller units were derived from it as multiples or subdivisions of 10.

1 metre = 10 decimetres = 100 centimetes = 1,000 millimetres
100 metres = 1km

Other basic units like *gram* for weight and *second* for time were established.

In 1889 the standard metre was redefined as the distance between two lines marked on a platinum-iridium rod preserved at a constant temperature of 273.16^0K at 1 bar pressure in the International Bureau of Weights and Measures at Severs, near Paris in France. All other metres are calibrated against it.

The other system of measurement is the *British System* according to which the standard of length is the *yard*. The standard yard for many years was a bronze bar exactly a yard long, kept with the British Government at a fixed temperature and pressure. In 1963 the yard was defined in terms of the metre (1 yard = 0.9144 metre). The British subdivision of the yard is:

1 yard = 3 feet   1 foot = 12 inches   1 mile = 5,280 feet

The basic units of weight and time in this system are *pound* and *second* respectively.

> **Try this**
> Why is the standard length kept at a fixed temperature and pressure? What is the effect of temperature on metals?

Check for expansion and contraction

1. Place two chairs against a table.
2. Pass a long copper wire through the loop of a pocket-knife. Fasten the ends of the wire to the back of the chairs. Keep the wire taut.
3. Heat the wire with a candle flame by moving the candle along the length of the wire. The wire will sag because of expansion due to heating.

4. Unwind the wire from the back of one chair and tie loosely so that the knife just touches the table.
5. Hold several ice cubes in a towel and run the ice along the length of the wire. The knife will leave the table as the wire shrinks due to cooling.

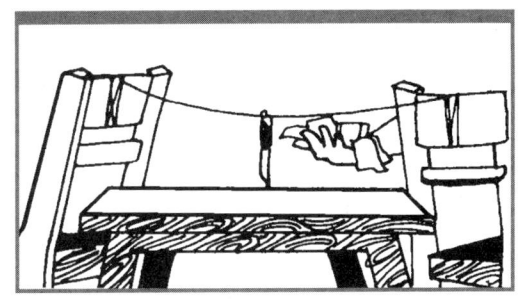

Because of the difficulty in preserving the exact length of the metre-bar, a new standard was agreed upon in 1960. This is based on the wavelength of the light emitted by atoms. This length never varies: the same atom under the same conditions always emits light of a fixed wavelength. The atom chosen for the purpose is of a gas called krypton-86. The metre is now defined as 1,650,763.73 wavelengths emitted by this atom under certain conditions.

Make your own ruler

You will need:
- a metal strip
- a wooden rod
- a broom stick
- a long rubber band
- a standard ruler
- a marker pen

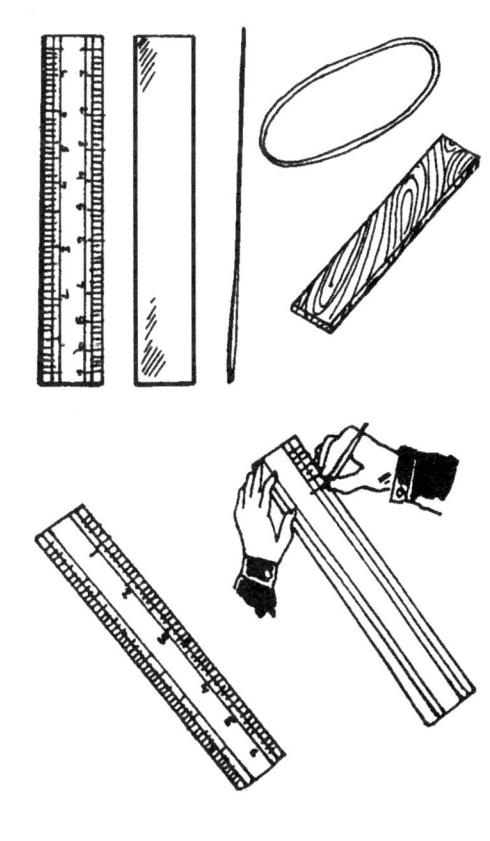

1. Taking the ruler as the standard of the rubber band, the broomstick, and the metal and wooden rods, so that you have four rulers.
2. Measure different lengths with the four rulers you made as well as the standard one. Which one do you think is best suited for measuring length?

Units used by scientists

Scientists all over the world use a system of measurement called the *International System of Units (ISI)*. Here we have seven basic units. They are:

   Metre (m) for length,
   Kilogram (kg) for mass,
   Second (s) for time,
   Kelvin (K) for temperature,
   Ampere (A) for electric current,
   Candela (cd) for light intensity and
   Mole (mol) for amount of substance.

Conversion of units

You should know how to convert from one system of unit to another as well as from one scale to another in the same system. This exercise will help you.

1. What is your weight in pounds? How much will you weigh in grams?
2. What is the height of this boy in metres, in inches, in miles?
3. A box has sides 2 dm long. What is its volume in cm^3?
4. How many seconds does a day have?

Some useful conversions

(You can add to this table.)

1 inch	=	2.54 cm
1 foot	=	0.3048 metres
1 mile	=	1.61 km
1 metre	=	39.4 inches
1 pound	=	0.45 kg
1 kg	=	2.2 pounds

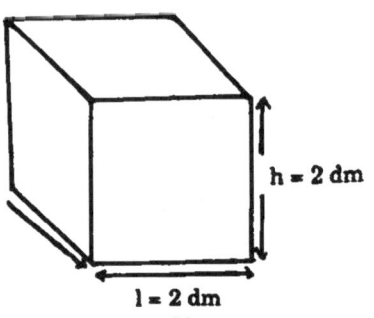

b = 2 dm
h = 2 dm
l = 2 dm = 20 cm

Volume = l x b x h

12

Length and Distance

Your idea of length

1. Here is a list of 10 things for you to do. Can you estimate the length of the following?
   a) Your height
   b) The height of your room
   c) The width of your bed
   d) The width of your bedroom door
   e) The distance from your house to school
   f) The length of the school ground
   g) The maximum distance between the fingers of your hand
   h) The radius of the pupil of your eye
   i) The length of a mosquito
   j) The thickness of your hair
2. What units have you used while estimating these lengths? Have you worked with the same unit? Why or why not?
3. Is it convenient to express the distance between your school and your house in cms, m or in kms?

A handy tool

When there is no ruler around, the following is a good way of measuring:

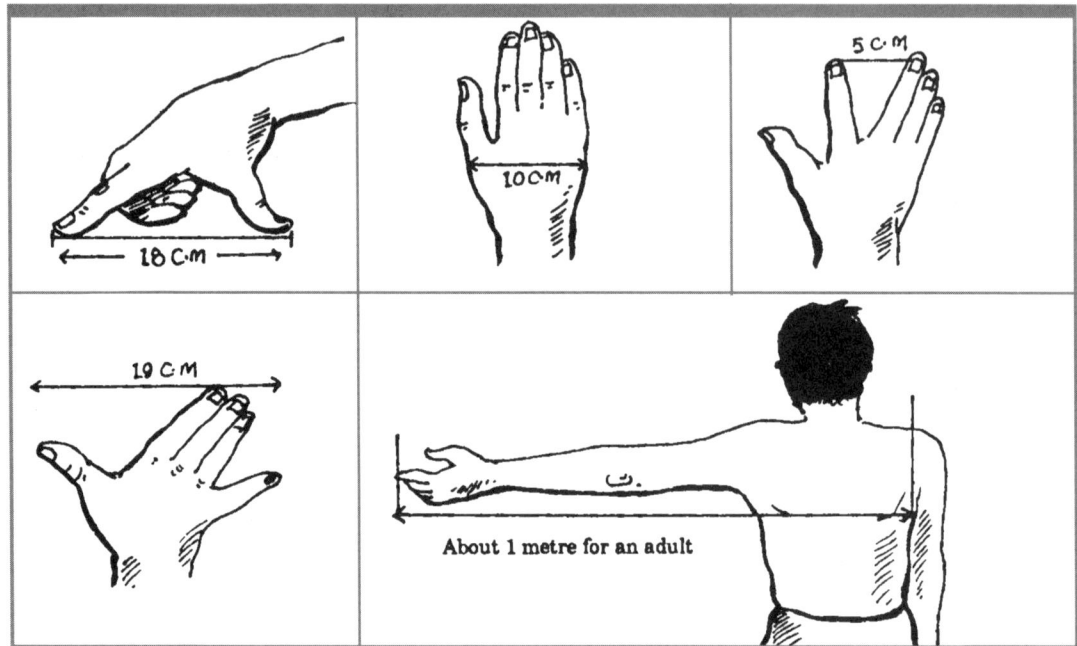

For longer distances, use your step or pace size. Measure your average step size as follows:

1. Mark out a stretch of 20 metres with a measuring tape.
2. See how many steps you need to cover the distance.

    It is possible that the result will be x steps plus a fraction. If the fraction is less than half, do not count it at all. If it is more than half count it as one more step.

3. Divide the number of steps by 20 metres to get your average step size in metres. Memorise the result.

To keep track of the number of steps when measuring long distances, count up to 10 and then bend one finger of the left hand. This means when all the fingers are bent, you have covered 50 steps. After every 50 steps, bend one finger of your right hand. Thus you can count up to 250 steps!

We find that the sizes of objects that interest us, vary widely. This table will give you a better idea.

Name of object	Picture	Range of length in metres
Nucleus		10^{-14}
Atom		10^{-10}
Thickness of a piece of paper		10^{-4}
Boy		1
Mountains		10^4
Distance of the sun from earth		10^{11}
Distance of the nearest star		10^{17}

10^2 is read as 10 to the power 2 and means 10×10.
$10^4 = 10 \times 10 \times 10 \times 10$
$10^{-4} = \frac{1}{10} \times \frac{1}{10} \times \frac{1}{10} \times \frac{1}{10} = .0001$

Accuracy in measurements

Industries need more accurate measuring devices than rulers. Machines have to fit together exactly. Measuring small lengths accurately also means that the scales should be divided into small units. You can check this easily.

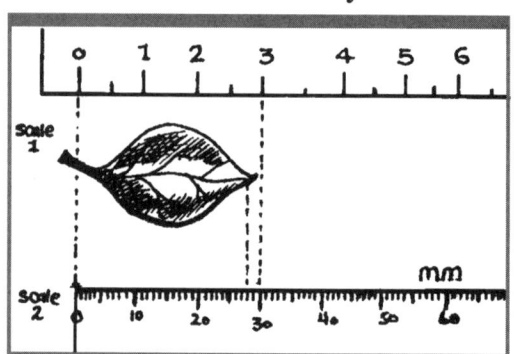

The picture shows two scales. Which one would you prefer to use to measure a small leaf?

Scale 1 gives a rough measurement of the leaf. Scale 2 is more accurate since it is divided into smaller units.

A better method of measuring small distances very accurately is by the *micrometer* or the screwgauge. It has a sleeve which rotates on a screw inside it. As the sleeve is rotated, it moves forward until the tip of the micrometer just touches the object being measured. The scale indicates the width of the object.

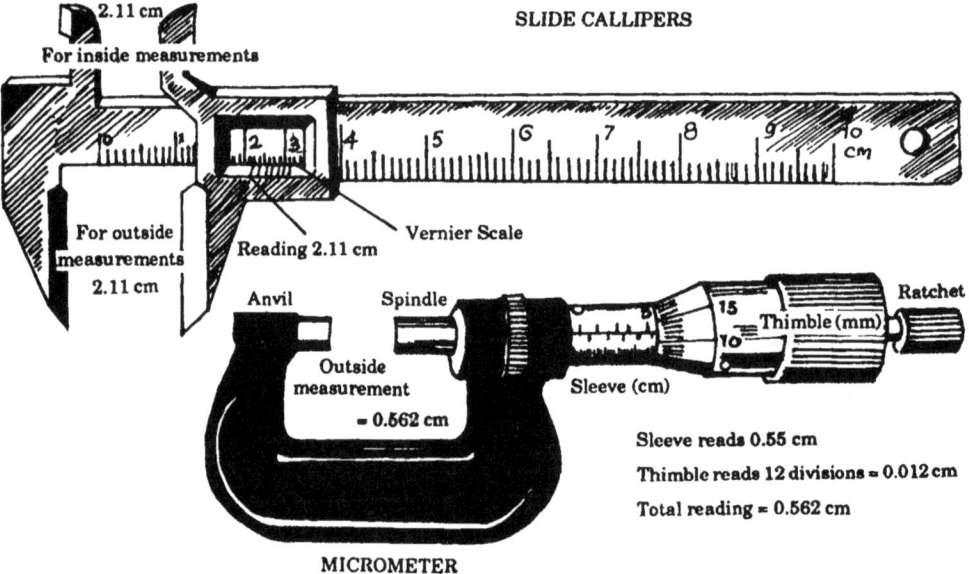

Slide Callipers are used for measuring diameters of tubes, rods, etc. The distance between the jaws of the callipers is read on a scale attached to the instrument. Notice that it has two sets of jaws, one for internal and other for external diameters.

Micrometers and callipers have their own limitations. They cannot be used for measuring objects of a size less than a millimetre.

The Use of a microscope

An ordinary optical microscope is used for 'looking' at tiny objects. Special microscopes are available which have scales fitted to them for measurement. The advantage of a microscope is that it magnifies the size of the object under inspection.

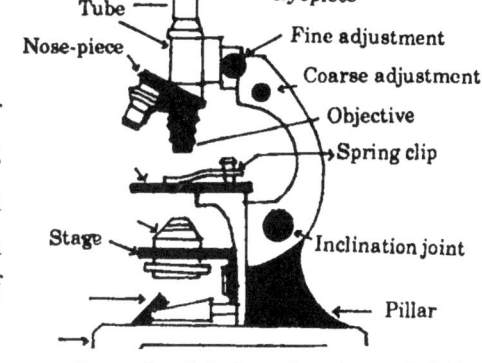

A microscope has two convex lenses. A convex lens is thicker in the middle than at the edges. A magnifying glass is nothing but a convex lens.

A homemade microscope

You will need:
- a magnifying glass
- a powerful convex lens from an old camera
- object to be studied

1. Place the camera lens close to the object under study. This is your objective.
2. The magnifying glass will serve as the eyepiece of your microscope. Hold the eyepiece close to your eyes. The distance between the eyepiece and the objective should be around 2 feet. Adjust the distance till you get an enlarged image of the object.

Measure the thickness of a page without a microscope

You will need:
- a book
- a ruler
- paper and pen

1. Count the number of pages of the book. It is better to choose a thick book.
2. Measure the thickness of the book (without the cover) with the help of a ruler.
3. If 500 pages measure, say, 5 cm, then 1 page must measure $^5/_{500}$ cm = .01 cm.

An optical microscope can measure lengths as small as 2×10^{-4} mm. That is real small indeed! But atoms and molecules are even tinier than this. For convenience, scientists use a smaller unit while measuring such small dimensions. This unit is called Angstrom (A^0).

$1A^0 = 10^{-10}$ metres.

To measure things of the order of Angstroms you need an electron or a tunnelling microscope.

Measure a molecule with a scale

You can make a very rough estimate of the size of a molecule in this way. Oil has large and complicated molecules made up of hydrogen, oxygen and carbon atoms. Cooking oil is usually a type of molecule called 'triglyceride'.

You will need:
- some cooking oil
- a small dish
- a wide glass
- water
- some talcum powder
- a thin wire
- a card
- sellotape
- a pair of scissors
- a ruler

1. Cut out a short length of wire and tape it in a loop to a small piece of card. Squeeze the end of the loop so that it encloses a space, roughly half a millimetre in width.
2. Fill the glass with water. Sprinkle a thin layer of powder on the water. Once covered completely, blow away excess powder.
3. Use the loop to pick up a drop of oil 0.5 mm across.

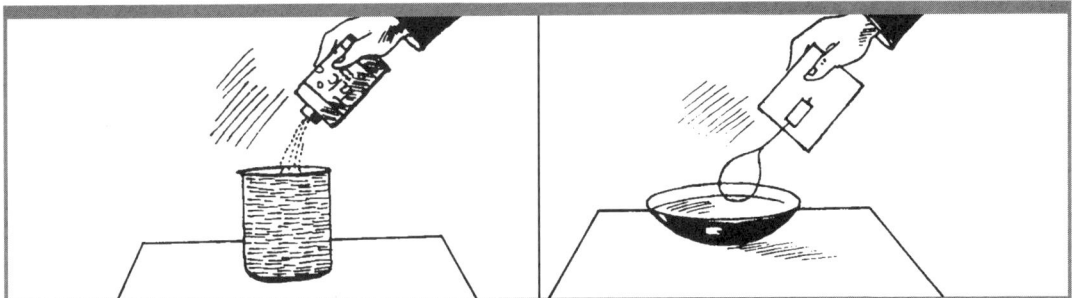

4. Lower the loop on to the water and open it carefully so that the oil drop spreads out over the water. Measure how far it spreads. Take an average of 4 measurements.

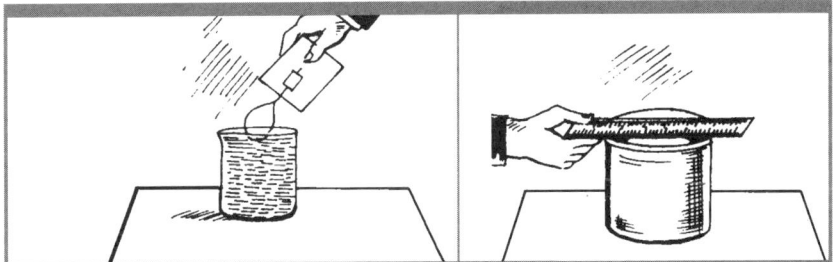

5. If you assume that the film of oil has one molecular thickness (t), then the size of the molecule can be calculated as:

$$t = \frac{1}{12d^2} \text{ mm, where } d = \text{diameter of oil film spread.}$$

Try this
How did we arrive at this formula? Remember that the volume of a cylinder of thickness t and diameter d is given by (t × d/4), while the volume of a sphere of diameter 0.5 is given by 4/3p (0.5/2)³.

Long distance measurements

Long distances, such as the height of a mountain or the distance between a planet and the earth, cannot obviously be measured directly with a tape. For this, 'angular measurements' are very useful.

If you look at the moon for some time, you will notice that its position shifts in the sky. We say the moon rises from the horizon and goes up. What changes the angle of view of the moon with respect to the plane of the horizon? This angle is called the 'elevation'. In fact every star in the sky can be given an angle of elevation according to its position in the sky.

Angular measurements help us to determine the sizes of astronomical objects. For example, you can measure the angular diameter of the moon, which is the angle subtended by the two diametrically opposite ends of the moon at a point on earth. Then, the diameter of the moon = (distance of the moon from the earth) × (angular diameter).

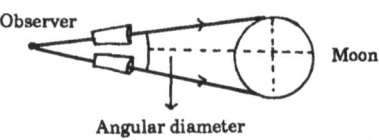

Angular diameter

1. Tape a strip of coloured paper on a wall.
2. Stand near the opposite wall and hold a pen in front of you so that the pen and the strip of paper are in a line.
3. Close your left eye and look at the pen. What do you observe?
4. Now close your right eye and look at the pen. What do you find?

We find that the position of the pen seems to shift with respect to the background depending on the position of viewing. This is called *parallax*.

The distance of the pen from the eyes can be found out approximately if you know the *angle* between the two lines of view and the distance (d) between the eyes. This is calculated from the relation,

$$S = d/Q$$

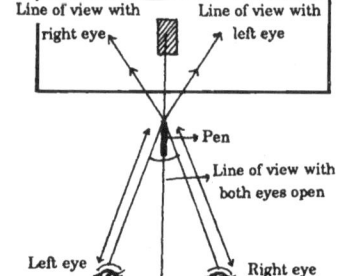

The formula becomes more and more exact as the distance between the observer and the object increases.

That is why parallax methods are commonly used to measure the distance of planets and stars. In this case the points of observation cannot be the left or right eye, but the two different observatories on earth. (Astronomical observatories are dome-shaped laboratories from where astrophysicists watch the sky with huge telescopes.)

A more convenient method is to look at the planet from the same observatory but at different times in the day and use the rotation of the earth about its axis to get the two points of observation. To determine the distance of a star, the earth's motion around the sun can be used and the star viewed of two different days in a year.

Astronomical scales

Astronomers usually measure distances in *light-years*. It is the distance travelled by light in one year.

The velocity of light is 300 million metres/sec. As there are 31.5 million seconds in one year, one light year is 9,460 million metres or about 6 million miles!

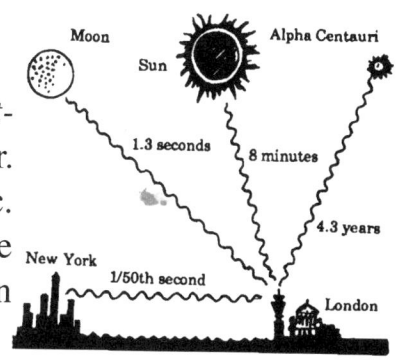

To appreciate how far the stars are from us, take a look at the picture.

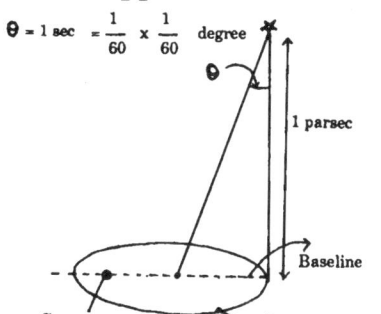

Another unit of length used frequently in astronomical measurements is the *parsec* (or parallactic second). It is the distance of an object that will show a parallax of 1 second of arc from opposite ends of a baseline equal to the distance from the earth to the sun.

1 parsec is 3.08×10^{16} metres.

You can have an estimate of how small these parallax angles are from the fact that the Star Alpha Centauri which is 4.29 light years away from the earth shows a parallax of only 2.64 seconds of arc when viewed from two locations of the earth six months apart.

The principal of an echo
A wave (be it a sound wave, an ultrasound wave, a radio or a light wave) bounces back or gets reflected when it hits an object.

Bounce the sound
1. Ask a friend to hold a smooth, big card or board on a table.
2. Arrange two cardboard tubes at an angle to the card, as shown. There should be a gap of about 6 cm between the card and the ends of the tubes.
3. Place an alarm clock at the outer end of one tube.
4. Put your ear to the end of the other tube. You can hear the clock tick even though the tubes are not connected. This is because the sound is reflected by the card.

This reflected sound is called an *echo*. The distance of the object can be assessed accurately by noting the time elapsed from the moment the signal is sent to the time the echo is received.

How far is the cliff?
Next time you are near a cliff, try to measure the distance between you and the cliff in this way:
1. Say the word "Go" loudly and note the exact time as you do so.
2. Check the time the moment you hear the first echo of "Go".
3. Do this several times and calculate the average time. This is the time taken by the sound waves of your voice to reach the cliff and come back. Therefore, half this time should be the time taken by the sound to reach the cliff. Multiply this with the speed of sound (330 metres/second) to find the distance between you and the cliff.

This principle of echo is widely used in measuring the distance at which aircrafts are as well as the distance between planets and stars. The wave used in this case is the radio wave and the instrument employed is a *Radar*.

Did you know that the name radar comes from the principle behind its operation, Radio Detection and Ranging (*RADAR*)?

Radars

The same principle applies to *SONAR* (Sound Navigation and Ranging). Ultrasonic waves are sent through water to detect the depth of oceans, submarines, etc.

In industry, ultrasound echoes are used to detect the position and depth of invisible flows inside a solid metal. The flow reflects an ultrasonic wave just as an underwater object would, and thus can be traced. This type of mechanical testing of material is useful because it is non-destructive.

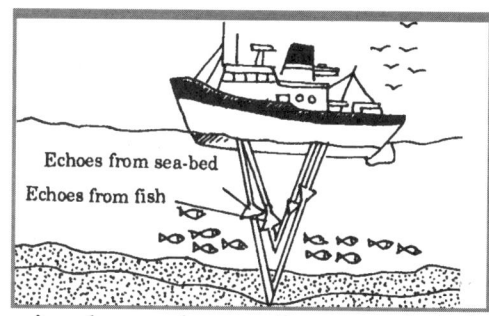
Echoes from sea-bed
Echoes from fish

Mass and Weight

We have, so far, used the words 'mass' and 'weight' as if they are interchangeable. But is it scientific to do so? Let us see.

You will need:
- a brick
- a block of wood of about the same size as the brick

1. Pick up the brick with one hand and the wood with the other. Which one feels heavier?
2. Which of the following statements are true?
    i) The brick has more weight than the wood.
    ii) The brick has more mass than the wood.
    iii) The brick has more matter the wood.
    iv) The earth is pulling the brick with a greater force.

All the four statements are true. Statements (i) and (iv) mean the same. The weight is the force with which the earth pulls the brick and the wood.

Statements (i) and (iv) can be explained by statement (ii). The earth pulls the brick with a larger force because the brick has more mass than the wood. Weight is the product of the mass of the body and the acceleration due to the gravity of the earth on the body.

Statements (ii) and (iii) are identical—*mass* is the quantity of matter contained in a body.

Hence, to a student of science, the weight of a brick of mass 1 kg is: 1kg weight or 9.8kg m/sec^2 (9.8 m/sec^2 is the acceleration due to the gravity of the earth). The unit of weight is kg m/sec^2. It is also called *Newton*.

The value of the acceleration due to gravity is different on different planets. The acceleration due to gravity on the moon is about $1/6^{th}$ of that on the earth. So you will weigh about 6 times lighter on the moon! However your mass will remain the same everywhere.

The masses of objects we come across in the universe have a wide range of values. At the lower end of the spectrum is the mass of an electron, which is 9.31×10^{-31} kg, whereas the mass of the known universe is estimated to be of the order of 10^{55} kg. You can get an idea of the range of masses from the values given in the table below.

Object		Mass (kg)
•	electron	10^{-30}
	atom	10^{-25}
	cell	10^{-10}
	man	10^{2}
	earth	10^{25}
	star	10^{30}

How do we measure mass?

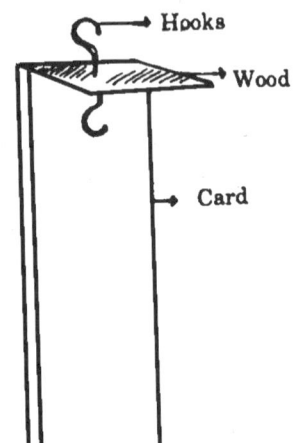

You will need:
- a spring
- 2 hooks
- a small square piece of wood
- a screw eyelet
- a piece of wire
- a card
- some weights
- sellotape
- a pen

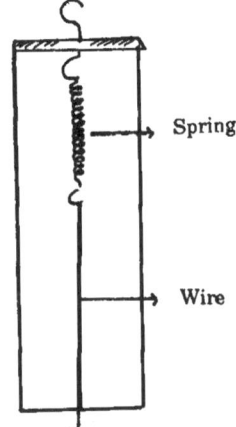

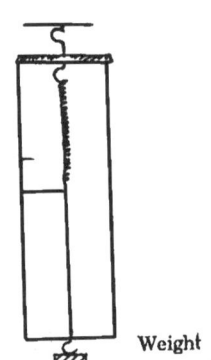

1. Fix the two hooks on the two sides of the wood.
2. Tape the card to the wood as shown.
3. Hang the spring from the lower hook.
4. Fix the screw eyelet to the bottom of the spring.
5. Attach the wire to the screw eyelet.
6. Mark the position of the spring on the card.
7. Hang weights from the wire and mark the elongation of the spring produced each time. Once you have the scale calibrated in terms of known masses, you can measure any mass with this arrangement.

This is called a *spring balance*. A spring balance actually measures the weight of a body. But we know that at a given place (ie, for a given acceleration due to gravity) the weights of to two objects are proportional to their masses. So we can get the mass of a body from a spring balance if the scale is calibrated in terms of mass.

A *common balance,* such as the one used by grocers, equalises or balances the weight of the object with that of standard weights to give the mass of the object. This is a two-pan balance. A single-pan balance has a scale calibrated in terms of standard weights. When you place an object on the pan, a pointer moves along the scale to show the weight.

Density

We know that different materials have different masses even if they are of the same size. The mass of a cube of iron of size 1cm × 1cm × 1cm = 1 cm³ is more than 1cm³ of sponge.

The lightness or heaviness of a substance for a given volume is called its *density.* 1cm³ of water weights 1 g. We say that the density of water is 1 g/cm³. The unit of density is g/cm³. The density of a substance depends on how tightly the molecules in the substance are packed. You can check this by the simple model given here.

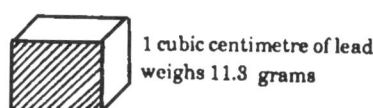
1 cubic centimetre of lead weighs 11.3 grams

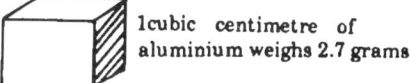
1cubic centimetre of aluminium weighs 2.7 grams

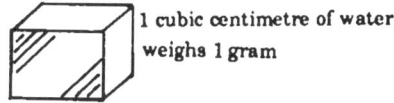
1 cubic centimetre of water weighs 1 gram

1. Take a small box. Feel its weight. The box is empty. Its density is low.
2. Put a layer of marbles in the box. Its density increases. Feel the increase in weight.
3. Repeat step 2 several times till the box is full. Now its density is the greatest. Note that the size of the box has remained the same throughout the experiment, but its mass increased each time you packed it with a layer of marbles.

Weighing the earth

I am sure you know that you cannot possibly weigh the earth like you weigh an apple. But its weight can be calculated if you know the force exerted by the earth on any body. We must thank Sir Isaace Newton for telling us that 'all bodies in this universe are attracted towards each other by a force of attraction which is proportional to their masses and the distance of separation between them.' This law holds for the earth (of mass M_E) and any body (of mass m) on the earth.

If written mathematically, it reads:

$$F = G \frac{M_E m}{R^2},$$

where, F = force of attraction between the two bodies
R = distance between the earth and the body, which is the radius of the earth for a body on the earth's surface
G = a constant, called the gravitational constant

We also know that the earth pulls all bodies with a force equal to the mass of the body (m) times the acceleration due to gravity (g).

Therefore, F = mg
Equating the two forces, you get,

$$G \frac{M_E m}{R^2} = mg$$

$$\text{or } ME = \frac{R^2 g}{G}$$

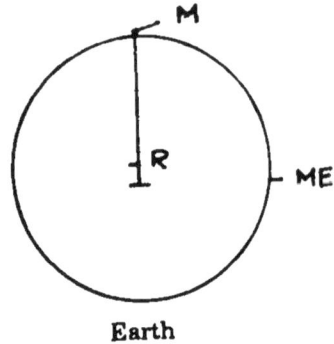

Earth

If you know the radius of the earth (R = 6.38 x 10⁶m) and the values of 'g' (9.8 m/sec²) and 'G' (6.67 x 10¹¹m³/kg. sec²) you can get the mass of the earth. The value of 'G' was first calculated by an English chemist, Henry Cavendish in 1798. So he is said to be the first person to weigh the earth!

Measuring Time

One of the first devices used to measure time was a sundial. As the sun spins on it axis, any shadow cast by the sun also moves round. This movement of the shadow was traced out and used for telling the time.

Check how a sundial works

You will need:
- a flowerpot
- a stick or rod
  (twice the height of the pot)
- a marker pen
- water

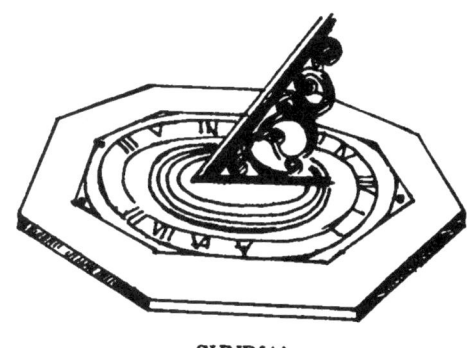
SUNDIAL

1. Place the flowerpot out in the sun in an upside down position.
2. Push the stick through the basehole of the pot and into the ground.
3. Mark the position of the shadow cast by the stick on the pot at intervals of 1 hour. Do this throughout the day. This is your sundial. You will be able to tell the time from the marks on your sundial on sunny days.
4. Will there be any change in the path of the shadow when you perform the experiment at different times of the year and at different places on the earth?

There are many problems with a timer like a sundial. It cannot give you time at night. Modifications are needed for a change in latitude and longitude.

Other methods of measuring time depend on processes that occur at regular rates — like the rate of falling of sand or water through a small hole.

Make your own sand timer

You will need:
- a small transparent bottle
- a sheet of paper
- some sand
- a marker pen
- a friend

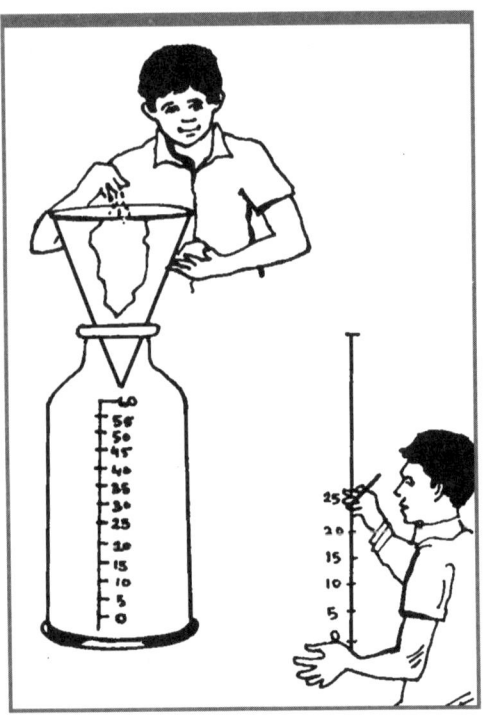

1. Fold the sheet to form a funnel with a small hole.
2. Put the funnel into the neck of the bottle.
3. Ask your friend to pour sand through the funnel.
4. As the sand starts falling, note the time, and after every 5 seconds mark the tip of the bottle. Do this for one minute.
5. Remove the sand from the bottle and draw the scale properly. This is a minute-clock. A larger version of this is called an hourglass.
6. Adjust the hole of the funnel and the time gap to get smaller or bigger scales.

Think it over

Our heart beats at regular intervals (the normal heartbeat is 72 pulses per minute). Why don't we use this as a timekeeper?

A discovery by the Italian scientist, Galileo Galilei in 1581 revolutionised the methods of the measurement of time. He timed the oscillations of a lamp hanging from a long chain in a church using his own pulse beat as a timer. Galileo found that time taken for a complete swing of the lamp did not depend on the extent of the swing, provided it was not too large. This was found to be true for any weight hung from a long string, as long as the length of the string remained fixed. Such a weight and string ensemble is called a *pendulum*.

Verify the law of the pendulum swing
1. Tie a weight to the end of a string and hang it from a hook. Let the string be half a metre long.
2. Make it swing gently, and time 10 swings (to and fro).
3. Increase the swing and time the next 10 swings. Is there any change in the two timings?
4. Change the weight. Does this alter the time of the swing?
5. Shorten and lengthen the string, and repeat steps 3 and 4. You will find that the time of the swing has reduced in the first case and increased in the second.

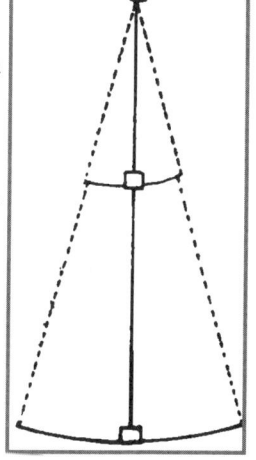

A pendulum about 25 cm long swings both ways in a second. A one-metre long pendulum takes roughly twice as long (about 2 seconds).

A Pendulum clock

Mechanical clocks had already started appearing in Europe since the 1300s. The discovery of the principle of the pendulum provided an impetus to the clock industry, and pendulum clocks were manufactured in the mid-1600s.

The early clocks were driven by falling weights. Portable clocks were made after spiral springs (mainsprings) began to be used in the fifteenth century. The pendulum was later replaced by a hairspring regulator.

Nowadays mechanical clocks and watches have been largely replaced by electronic ones. An electronic watch uses a quartz crystal as a time regulator. Quartz has a peculiar property. It can be made to vibrate at a precise frequency of 32, 768 vibrations per second when a small current is passed through it. This is done in a *digital watch*. Electronic circuits in the watch reduce this frequency in stages to one vibration per second, and this is then used to drive a digital display that shows the time.

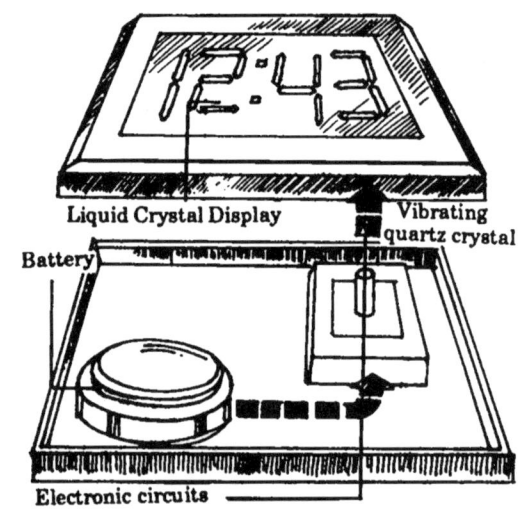

For precise measurements of time, scientists use quartz-controlled clocks that are calibrated against *atomic clocks*. An atomic clock is regulated by the frequency of radiation from atoms of caesium-133.

Did you know?
The standard atomic clock varies by only one second in 1,000 years, while a quartz crystal does so every 3 years and the pendulum clock every 3 months.

Temperature

Temperature is a measure of how hot or cold something is. On a cold day the temperature of the air is lower than on a hot day. Ice has a very low temperature, while boiling water has a high temperature. The temperature of the sun is very high.

We can measure the temperature of an object in many ways. One way is to touch things with our hands and feel how cold or hot they are. Let us see how reliable this is.

Check your temperature sense

You will need:
- a pan of hot water
- a pan of ice-cold water
- a pan of lukewarm water

1. Put the three pans of water on a table.
2. Put both your hands in the lukewarm water and hold them there for half a minute. Do both your hands feel the same temperature?
3. Now, place your left hand in the hot water and your right hand in the icy water for a minute.
4. Quickly dry your hands and plunge them both in the lukewarm water. How do your hands feel? What do you think is the temperature of the water? What do you think of your sense of temperature?

For accurate measurements of temperature we use *thermometers*. There are many different types of thermometers. Ordinary thermometers use a liquid, either mercury or alcohol, which increases in volume when heated and contracts when cooled.

A clinical thermometer, that you use for measuring fever, uses mercury. When you put in your mouth, the mercury expands and goes up the tube. When it is removed, the mercury contracts but it cannot flow back through the narrow kink at the neck. This leaves the mercury in the stem, showing your temperature. You have to shake the thermometer to get all the mercury back into the bulb.

A household thermometer contains alcohol. Alcohol has no colour. So a red dye is added to make it visible.

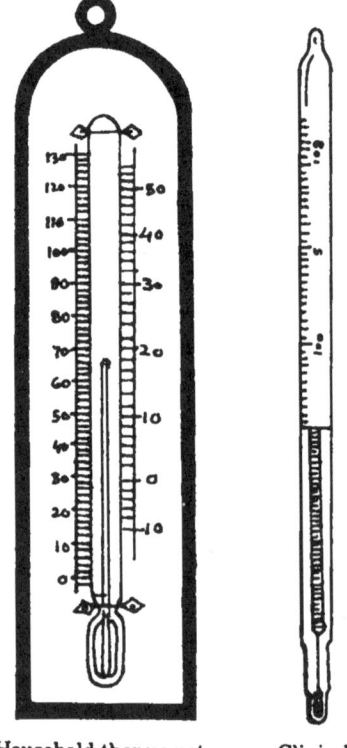

Household thermometer   Clinical thermometer

These are called liquid-in-glass thermometers. Note the markings or graduations along the glass tube of the two thermometers. Can you account for the difference?

Thermometers like the bimetallic thermometer, the thermocouple thermometer and the digital thermometer are also in use.

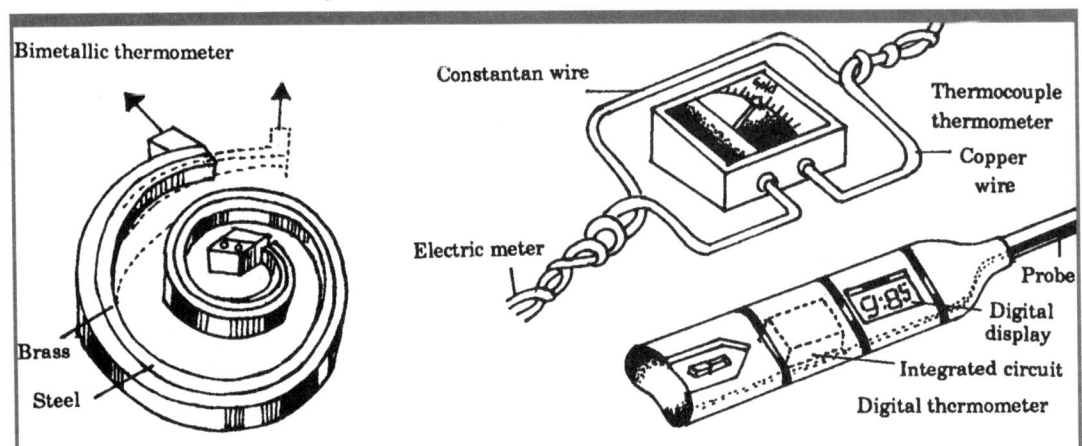

Temperature scales

There are three standard scales of markings for measuring temperature. On the *Celsius,* or the Cetigrade scale (°C), the temperature at which water freezes, is 0°C and at which water boils is 100°C. These are called the lower fixed point and the upper fixed point. On the *Fahrenheit scale,* the freezing point of water is 32°F and its boiling point is 212°F. The other scale, used for scientific measurements, is called the *Kelvin scale.* On this scale, the lowest possible temperature, called absolute zero, is zero°K. 1°K is equal to 1°C. On the Kelvin scale, 0°C becomes 273°K and 100°C is 373°K.

Think it over

When you say your body temperature is 100, which temperature scale are you referring to?

Convert from °C to °F

1. Look for the temperature chart of various places in the world in your newspaper.
2. Note the hottest and the coldest places.
3. What is the temperature scale used in the chart?
   If it is in °C, can you convert it to °F?
   Apply the formula: $$\frac{t°C}{100} = \frac{t°F - 32}{180}$$

[This is true because a 100° rise in temperature in the centigrade scale corresponds to a 180° rise in the Fahrenheit scale.]

Make an air thermometer

You will need:
- a used electric bulb
- a one-holed rubber stopper with a 60 cm glass tubing (get it from the chemistry laboratory) – the stopper must fit tightly into the neck of the bulb
- a candle
- a wooden stand (make it if you don't have one)
- a piece of paper
- a bottle of water
- ink
- a thermometer
- nails and adhesive

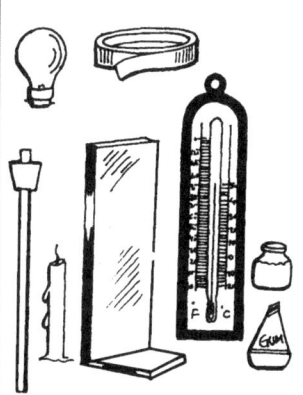

1. Fit the stopper into the neck of the bulb. Seal it by dropping some wax from the candle around the joint. This is your thermometer.
2. Paste the paper on the inside vertical face of the wooden stand.
3. Colour the water in the bottle with a little ink. Dip the glass tube of the thermometer in the ink-water.
4. Fix the thermometer to the stand.
5. Now heat the bulb of the thermometer gently with the candle to drive out some of the air. Drive out just enough air to ensure that when the bulb cools to room temperature, the coloured water will rise about half way up the tube.
6. To mark your scale, attach the other thermometer next to your air thermometer. Put the stand out in the sun for an hour.
7. At the end of an hour, make a line on the paper at the level of the water, and mark the reading of the thermometer at this point.
8. Repeat steps 6 to 7 in a cool, dark place.
9. Divide the space between the two marks into equal divisions and mark off the corresponding temperatures. Did you notice that this is an inverted thermometer?

Testing a thermometer

Can you find out whether the graduation of your thermometer is correct or not? To do this:
1. Take a laboratory thermometer and note the 0°C and the 100°C marks.
2. Set some water to boil and dip the thermometer in it. When the water boils, note how closely the mercury registers 100°C or 212°F. This is how you check the upper fixed point.
3. To check the lower fixed point, dip the thermometer in a blow of ice. After some time check whether the mercury really shows 0°C or 32°F.

Remember that this experiment will give right readings only at sea-level or where the barometer reading is 760mm of mercury.

Electrical Measurements

Scientists and engineers use a wide variety of electrical instruments for measuring and recording experimental data. Most electrical instruments measure either current (rate of flow of electricity) or voltage (electrical 'pressure difference').

The standard instrument used for detecting currents flowing in a circuit is the *Galvanometer*.

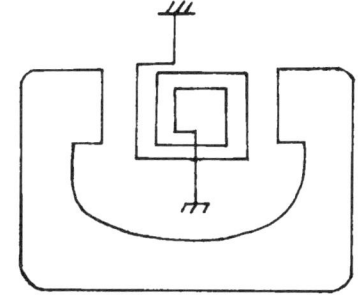

A rectangular coil consisting of many turn of fine wire is placed between the north and south poles of a horseshoe magnet. The coil is free to rotate about the vertical line along the XY direction.

When a current flows through the coil, a magnetic field is set up. This magnetic field interacts with the field of the horseshoe magnet, and the coil is forced to turn.

If a pointer is attached to the coil, it will indicate the level of current on a marked scale.

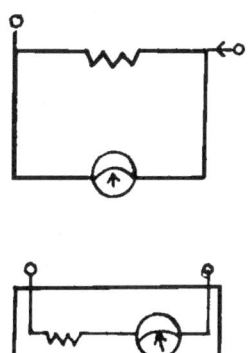

A Galvanometer fitted to a resistance across its terminals is called an *ammeter* (amp-meter). An ammeter measures currents in units of *amperes*.

A *voltmeter* which measures voltage in units of *volts* can be made from a galvanometer with a resistance connected in series with it.

Make a galvanometer

You will need:
- a magnetic compass
- a 9-volt battery
- a block of wood 4" × 5" × 1"
- the cover of a small cardboard box
- 4 board pins
- 2 paper clips
- some insulated wire

1. Wrap about 10 turns of the insulated wire around the cardboard.
2. Scrape the insulation from the wire ends.
3. Place the cardboard on the block of wood and secure it in place with board points. Do not push the pins completely down.
4. Wrap the ends of the wires around two board pins.
5. Bend the paper clips in half. Slip the clips under the pins and push the pins firmly down.
6. Place the magnetic compass inside the lid of the box.
7. Connect two wires to the two terminals of the battery. Fix one of these wires to one clip.
8. Touch the other paper clip with the second wire. What do you observe? The compass needle moves, showing that there is a magnetic field around. A flow of current through the wires creates this magnetic field.
   If a scale could be attached to the compass, you could actually measure current.

Avometer

The instrument which is widely used in laboratories for electrical measurements has scales for measuring current, voltage and resistance. It is called an ampere-volt-ohm meter, or an *Avometer (ohm* is the unit of resistance).

Ammeters and voltmeters can also be used indirectly to measure non-electrical quantities, such as pressure, rate of flow and temperature. This is possible as these quantities can be suitably converted, or transduced, into electrical current and voltage.

Temperature is measured electrically by a platinum resistance thermometer. The resistance of platinum changes appreciably with temperature. So the current passed through a platinum wire (which is proportional to the resistance) varies according to the temperature.

INDEX

Acceleration, 6
Ammeter, 37, 39
Avometer, 38
Cavendish Henry, 28
Cubit, 9
    — royal, 9
Density, 6
Force, 6
Galilei Galileo, 31
Galvanometer, 37, 38
International Bureau of Weights and Measures, 10
International System of Units, 12
Kelvin, 7, 35
Krypton-86, 11
Libra, 9
Light year, 21
Metric system 10
Micrometer, 16
Microscope, 17, 18
    — Optical, 18
Millipassus, 9
Parallactic second, 21
Parallax, 20, 21
Pendulum, 31
Power, 6
RADAR, 23
Screwgauge, 16
Slide Callipers, 16
SONAR, 23
Spring balance, 26
Thermometer, 8, 34
    — bimetallic, 34
    — clinical, 7
    — digital, 34
    — household, 34
    — platinum resistance thermometer, 39
    — thermocouple, 34
Ultrasonic waves, 23
Voltmeter, 37, 39
Volume, 6
Watch,
    — atomic, 32
    — digital, 32